FACE OFF

BEHIND THE MASK

HELEN ROYSTON

DEDICATION

To My Spiritual Parents: Overseers of Ministers For Christ

Bishop Richard & Prophetess Louise Holman

When I Came To Myself

"But when he came to himself, he said, 'How many of my father's hired servants have bread enough and to spare, and I perish with hunger! I will arise and go to my father and will say to him, "Father, I have sinned against heaven and before you, and I am no longer worthy to be called your son. Make me like one of your hired servants.

But when he was still a great way off, his father saw him and had compassion!

Hello. You owe me! In case I'm not here when this book is published.

The Bishop

Sat, Nov 16, 2019

I ONCE WAS LOST BUT NOW I'M FOUND

ACKNOWLEDGMENTS

I give honor to my Father in Heaven who knew me before I was in my mother womb. Who pulled me out of darkness into the light. This book wouldn't have been possible without Him.

To my parents Freddie Ray Tolliver & Henry Miles who raised me to be the Woman I am today. To my extended family.

I owe an enormous debt of gratitude to my Spiritual Parents, Overseers of Ministers for Christ Christian Center, the Late Bishop Richard Holman and Prophetess Louise Holman.

To My Bishop, who pushed me into writing this book under Richard L. Holman Ministries Inc.,

To my MFC Family, who I truly love with everything in me.

To all of the people that helped me become the person I am today.

A Special Thanks to the Publishing Company and Editor of Full Bloom Publishing, Bishop Connie Stewart for making this project a reality in the earth realm.

To my Pushers who pushed me to the next level that wanted to see me walk into my purpose. The two that picked me up in the spirit and threw me out of the boat. To the one who road this wave with me and cheered me on through all the birthing pains.

To Pastor Charmaine Brooks who has always been there for me from the beginning, praying for me and this book.

_____

To The Love Of My Life

My Family

My Husband Gregory Royston Jr., my love, my partner for 25 years.

My Son Paris Watson, my Daughter Britian Royston, my Daughter Asia Royston, my Son Gregory Royston III and my Daughter Miracle Royston

Table of Contents

INTRODUCTION

In 2012 I left the church after being a member since I was fifteen yrs. old. When I left the church my husband and five kids went with me. I went from church to church and could not eat everything. The sheep knows the shepherd's voice and when I no longer heard the voice, I knew I was a sheep lost outside of the pasture. Searching for the voice and could not find it. I brought this on myself walking in disobedience and pride. I pulled myself from under the covering of my shepherds and went on a journey without a sail with no direction. I thought I was doing the right thing by God, but I was really walking in rebellion. I was sick and afraid, but I did not let them know. So, I covered my face with makeup and pretended to be something I was not at the time. One day I was at my husband's grandmother's house and my mother-n- law was getting ready for church that evening. I was acting like I didn't care but, on the inside, I really wanted to go. She said you should go with me to church tonight, they are having a revival. I said oh no, I am not going to that church. I thought about it and thought until I gave in. Now let me remind you, I was a leader in the church, so I sat on the front row, but I walked through the door and went straight to the back and sat on the last pew. I was always taught to do what you know to do and not what you want. I was so ashamed and embarrassed. I thought people were judging me and that my leaders were angry with me because they didn't say anything, only to realize they were happy to see me come back home. When you are out of the will of God it opens a door for the enemy to come in and mess with your mind. Psalm 69:5 O God, You know my foolishness; And my sins are not hidden from You. That tells me that I cannot simply put on a mask and hide my guilt from God. Sitting back there, I heard the Lord say, I want to touch the real you, Take the Mask Off! FACE-OFF! Write the book.

CHAPTER 1

My Early Childhood Years

I will never forget my early childhood years. As you know childhood has memories that were exciting and not so exciting, but they never seem to leave you. My mother and I always had a good and close relationship. She did the best she could raising my brother and me. She was a single mother and worked for the school district driving buses. She made sure we stayed in school and had the things we needed. We didn't seem to want for anything. Though we grew up in a one-bedroom apartment, we always had everything we needed. At that time (as a child), it didn't seem to me that we were struggling. I was taught at an early age how to cook and clean up the house. Mother taught us how to be responsible and how to keep up the house when she was away at work. We would lock up the house when she left for work and lock ourselves in when we got back from school. She taught us how to get on the bus when she was away, and all the necessary things that young children needed to know when there was no father in the home to protect them.

Holidays were fun for us, especially during Christmas time. The house would be full of toys and the smell of mama's good ole' cakes and pies & ****. It seems like we had everything

we wanted or could even imagine. My mother would cook so much food during those times, it seemed like she was cooking for everyone in the neighborhood. During Easter time we would have huge baskets full of toys and candy. Easter was a special time for me because that was the day my mother would go to church. She would dress my brother and me from head to toe, and you couldn't tell us anything. We were sharp as a tack. I would have on my big dress with ruffle socks and sparkling shoes, … I mean she did it BIG! After church, we would eat a big meal and sit down to look at the Ten Commandments

I remember growing up as a little girl, going to see my father on weekends was so exciting for me. My father owned this green station wagon and every Sunday my father would load us up in the station wagon and take us to church. My brother and I would sit in the very back of the car playing on our way to church. My father was a Deacon at his church, he worked the front door. My brother and I would sit in the back of the church by the door where my father was working. He made us sit there very quietly to listen to the preacher. If we tried to fall asleep, he would pop us in the back of our heads and tell us we didn't come to church to sleep. After church, we would go back to my father's house and eat some good soul food that he prepared the day before. My father would walk around the house with his hands lifted, praying. He had bibles open all around the house. We didn't look at TV, we only listened to music. His favorite song was Jesus Help your Children. When I was 7 years old, my brother and I lived with my mom in an apartment complex. At the end of the apartments was a church called Greater Friendship MBC, Pastor Golf was the Pastor. As a child, I would get up early on Sunday morning to get my brother and myself ready for church. We would leave out early to make it to Sunday school on time. I learned my first bible scripture John 3:16. at that church. I remember sitting at the front of the church, I loved to hear the Pastor call on the name of Jesus. It was something about the name Jesus. I was not scared of him; it was very comforting like something would come over me. After Pastor Golf would preach, he would say, sister Tolliver, come give us a selection. I was 7 years old when I accepted Jesus as my Lord.

As I grew up, things started to change. I started getting into a lot of trouble and hanging with the wrong crowd. I began to act out by skipping school in my high school years. My mother tried her best to get me some professional help, but it didn't work. My relationship with her started declining when I was about 16 years old. During this time, she took me to a psychiatric hospital and just dropped me off. I didn't understand then what was going on with her and why she did that to me, but I do seem to understand now. At the time I was so hurt and angry from her doing that to me. I felt lonely and cold. I was in that place all by myself, in my own little world, asking myself over and over. What's going on with me. How did I end up in this place, and why me?

I believe this experience is what pivoted me to a place of no return, that is, in my mind. I felt abandoned, lonely, rejected, and I was very afraid. I felt like I was all by myself. I shut myself down. My failure to ask questions placed me on a dark path. It would take the prayers of A FEW TO HOLD ME UP. Life hit me so hard I didn't know which way to go. I was hurting on the inside and afraid of everything because of the hand I had been dealt. I felt powerless, I even cried myself to sleep, I had many mixed emotions. But the saying is every dark tunnel has light and hope. These were real feelings for me at this moment. Many children are dealing with the same thing right now. I didn't know what was going to happen to me next. All I could think over and over, is, why did she do this to me? How did I get to this place? When will this ever end? Even though I felt like I was at a place of no return, God always have a way of hiding me and keeping me.

Growing up as a Teenager

Growing up as a teenager I experienced some tragic things in my life. At the age of thirteen, a friend of the family molested me. I remember going over to my step-sister's house to help her with her son's birthday party. That night about 1:00 am, I went to the restroom and her husband came in on me. He took my arm and put it behind my back and said, "If you make a sound, I'm going to break your arm." As he continued, tears began to roll down my face. On the inside, something inside of me was just calling on Jesus. This was the most hurt and scariest feeling of my life. I remember getting back in the bed waiting on him to go back to sleep so I could escape. After he fell asleep, I jumped up and ran out of that house so fast, I didn't realize that I didn't have any shoes on my feet. I just kept on running and I didn't stop until I got to my house. When I got to the top of the stairs (at our apartment), out came a loud cry, "Help me, Help me," as I banged on the door. My mom opened the door with her shotgun ready to kill whoever was in the way. A month later, I found out I was pregnant. This was very devastating to me.

I was torn between the decision of my grandmother and my mother about what to do about the baby. My grandmother wanted me to have the baby, but my mother wanted me to have an abortion. A few days later, there I was sitting in front of the doctors listening to them explain to me all of the different tools they could use to kill someone inside of me. At the same time, I felt like I was dying myself. I really don't know how I made it through that period of my life. All I can say is, "There had to be a God somewhere who cared about me" because I don't know how I made it through that.

Dealing with Peer Pressure

Peer pressure was hard for me to deal with. I never understood as a child why my friends would play with me one day and the next day they would say, "Let's not play with Jeanette today." This didn't seem to sit right with me when it first started happening, so as I continued to grow older, I did whatever it took just to have friends. I was a leader in my own right but at the same time, I was a follower because I didn't want to be left out. As a child I knew I was set apart for something, I just didn't know what it was. I always wanted to be a part of something or someone. When people asked me to do something I just did it. As my life progressed and I met new friends, I started drinking and partying. I was introduced to drugs and all kinds of terrible things while in high school. All we would do is skip school and get high all day and night. I lived a very dark life. My life was out of control. My mother couldn't deal with me anymore. From getting help through counselors to taking medication, nothing would work. But do you know God still had a plan for my life? Yes, he had a plan even in the darkest moments of my life and my mother's life.

There was a teacher that supported me in middle school. She would take out the time to work with me during school hours. She would always tell me I was great; she saw something in me that I didn't see in myself. After all, she taught a behavioral class full of bad kids. This class was called BAC (Behavior Adjustment Class). I sat in the back of everybody and everything. Yes, I was in that class, and I was ashamed, and yes, I rode on the little bus, yes, the little yellow bus. You know the bus people use to talk about, I was on that one. That teacher's name was Ms. Gosset. She knew how to bring out the best in me. How she did it, I have no idea, but she did. I really believe it truly takes a village to raise one child. Well for me it did. It was this same woman that my mother called to tell her she couldn't do anything else with me, that I was out of control. Ms. Gosset agreed to help my mother by allowing me to stay with her for a while. Ms. Gossett is a faith walker. Again, on this journey, everyone went to church in her house. God always finds a way of returning you back. Oh yes, Sunday morning at First Outreach the Late Pastor Richardson, a house full of Love. This is where I met my Shepherds, the late Bishop Richard Holman and Prophetess Louise Holman my Overseers of Ministers For Christ Christian Center. I guess I was too much for Ms. Gosset to handle and she did what she could. She introduced my Pastor to me, and they took me like family. After moving back home with my mother, she decided to take me to their house and drop me off. Mother (Prophetess Holman) introduced me to her cousin Rose Rita that took me into her home and loved me like I was one of her own, three boys and myself. Wow, my mother searched all over for help, each person she reached out to played a very important part in my life. I am, because of them. Every person she reached out to put me back in the face of God. Do you really know that God has a great plan for your life? At that time, I did not know that, but now I know.

God has a great plan for your life. He is bringing you out of the back scenes. What you think is hurting you is really helping you. The people you think do not understand you, are the ones pushing you forward. All things work together for the good of those who love God, to those who are thee called according to His purpose. You are Thee Called with Purpose. Let's fast forward about me today. I have five kids; each one has dealt with something in their life growing up. For me to look at the oldest to the youngest, I am reminded God is a God of turnaround. The things the oldest used to do, he does not do them anymore. He has entered another phase in his life, from a boy to a man. For many years he was masked up, hurting on the inside and smiling on the outside. From day one it was a struggle for him. He lost oxygen from his brain when he was born. The doctor said he would never walk. He was called slow in school and gay by others. He was told he would never graduate. God is a God of a turnaround. What the devil meant for your bad, God meant it for your good. My son will be 25 years old this year. He's walking, he's a high school graduate, and he loves women. Every negative word that was spoken to him, he worked hard to prove them wrong. He was willing to face his pain and say pain, you will not have power over me. Yes, you have to put some work in. You must invest in yourself and most importantly you must forgive. Remember forgiveness is not for the other person, it's really for you. You are forgiving others to free yourself. Maya Angelou once said: "It's one of the greatest gifts you can give **yourself**, to **forgive**. **Forgive** everybody." One of the greatest gifts was given to us freely with a great price tag that no man can match. Jesus paid the price that we may live only

7

if we receive and believe, then he will take our sins and know them no more. That gift lives in us too, we just have to know it and use it. Once you learn how to use your gift, your gift will free you.

What Did Your Childhood Look Like?

_____
_____
_____
_____
_____
_____
_____
_____
_____
_____
_____
_____
_____
_____
_____
_____
_____
_____
_____
_____
_____
_____
_____
_____
_____
_____
_____
_____
_____
_____
_____

How Did Your Environment Shape The Way You Treat Others?

_____
_____
_____
_____
_____
_____
_____
_____
_____
_____
_____
_____
_____
_____
_____
_____
_____
_____
_____
_____
_____
_____
_____
_____
_____
_____
_____
_____
_____

What Are Some Things You Would Need To Forgive Others For?

_____
_____
_____
_____
_____
_____
_____
_____
_____
_____
_____
_____
_____
_____
_____
_____
_____
_____
_____
_____
_____
_____
_____
_____
_____
_____
_____
_____
_____
_____

List Ten Steps You're Willing To Take In Order To Heal?

_____

_____

_____

_____

_____

_____

_____

_____

_____

_____

_____

_____

_____

_____

_____

_____

_____

_____

_____

_____

_____

_____

_____

_____

_____

_____

_____

_____

_____

What's Your Testimony?

What Steps Did You Take To Overcome Your Faults Or Short Comings?

_____

_____

_____

_____

_____

_____

_____

_____

_____

_____

_____

_____

_____

_____

_____

_____

_____

_____

_____

_____

_____

_____

_____

_____

_____

_____

_____

_____

List 10 Ways To Become A Better You

_____

_____

_____

_____

_____

_____

_____

_____

_____

_____

_____

_____

_____

_____

_____

_____

_____

_____

_____

_____

_____

_____

_____

_____

_____

_____

_____

_____

_____

_____

CHAPTER 3

Knowing God for Myself

I knew God to be a healer after hemorrhaging during the birth of my last child when the doctor came into the room to say, there is nothing I can do, just pray. From that day until now I'm still here and my daughter Miracle is sixteen yrs. old, thriving! Five years ago, my husband was diagnosed with sarcoidosis with half of a lung on both sides because lesions were eating them away! He is still here thriving and breathing with a new set of lungs the Lord gave him! My Father is a Miracle Worker and a Promise Keeper, I Give Him Glory! He has touched my life in many ways and healed my body and my mind, putting my past behind me.

God will put people in your life to get you to a certain place in your life. People who can identify your purpose and see the real you. He will put people in your life to help you see what you don't see. God will send people to confirm what has been spoken over you and push you in place. I call that the special project. I thank God for the Late Bishop Richard Holman that saw something in me that I didn't see in myself. He loved God's people so much he was willing to pour himself out. He wasn't selfish with what God gave him; he was always looking for the opportunity to impart into someone else. He was a great administrator, a great teacher, and a great trainer! All the years of his training and I did not get it until God called him home. I was hearing him and getting the download of information, but the transfer did not take place until God called him to rest. Now I can hear his voice so clearly. It is a privilege to sit under a great teacher, however, it was not easy with The Bishop. He would always get on me about something and mother would say, Bishop, leave that girl alone and he would say First Lady she knows better. I remember a month or two before he passed, Bishop and Pastor were running behind as well as Pastor Murray and his wife. It was a little before 11:15, almost time for the service to start. I called and texted to get the instructions and no answer. I called and texted the senior Pastors and no answer. At this time, the church was full of people, and I had to make a decision. Do I wait to hear back from Bishop or Pastor Murray, or do I start the service? My heart was beating so fast, I felt like I was about to pass out, but the people didn't know. Everybody was looking at me, Royston what are we going to do. At that moment, I heard the instructions do what you know to do. Everybody was in position waiting on the green light from me. I went to the pulpit and started the service. While the Praise & Worship was going, I kept looking at the door thinking to myself, I may have to bring the word. It was really over for me at this point. I was put on the spot to do the whole service if I had to do it scared, but people didn't know, and I was ready. Then the doors opened, Bishop, Prophetess, and the Senior Pastor came into the building. My, my, my, my, the angels in heaven were singing in my ear. I was saying to myself thank you Lord even though I was scared and nervous. This was just a test to see if I could handle and carry out what I knew. The Bishop was hard on his children, but it pushed us into the presence of God. He was determined, it was God or nothing.

During my time of grieving, I felt like I lost my way with God until I came into the presence of the Lord. I didn't know what direction to go in, because the person I followed for years had now left the scene. It was also at that moment my eyes were opened. I saw the Lord and His train filled my house so much that I went into a place of repentance. I came face to face with reality, what I was doing and what I wasn't doing. The encounter I had with the Lord was like the fork in the road, it was a turning point for me. I knew at that moment I had to get it right now or I was going to die! My Life was on the line and many people were depending on me. We only have one life to live and then comes judgment. I don't want to leave here for the Lord to tell me, depart from me I never knew you. I cried out to the Lord, he heard my cry, and he came in and gave me comfort. It was me and God, My Healer, My Provider, My Protector, My Way Maker, My Peace, right there with me. God came in and dealt with all my pain, my issues, and hurts. He pulled the sheets back where I was hiding. God fully uncovered me and exposed those unclean spirits that were tormenting me for years and years all the way down throughout my generations, for nothing is hidden from the Lord. He began to deliver and heal me on the inside. Then the Holy Spirit came into my life and washed, cleansed, renewed me, and give me a new life

Know God for yourself so He can transform you. So, you can walk in newness and breathe again. Ezekiel 36: 25-27 reads, I will sprinkle clean water on you, and you shall be clean of all your uncleanness. I will remove the heart of stone from your flesh and give you a heart of flesh. And I will put my Spirit within you and cause you to walk in my statutes and be careful to obey my rules. All you must do is surrender. I can say surrender all day and nothing happens, but you will know when your surrender day comes. God's plan for our life is so perfect. He said I wish above all things that you prosper and be in good health, even as thy soul prospers. He wants to give you good health, remove all sickness and diseases. Meaning, He wants you to experience Him in such a way it would blow your mind. A place of peace that passes everybody's understanding. A relationship with you and God. He wants to take your pain and turn it into treasures.

There's nothing like your change being seen and hearing others speak of your newness. Now you become the center of attention, all eyes on you because of your change. Paul says in John 3 I was most happy when some friends arrived and brought the news that you persist in following the way of Truth. Nothing could make me happier than getting reports that my children continue diligently in the way of Truth! God wants us to walk in truth! That's it right there, truth. Wake up every morning, look at yourself in the mirror, and say, Come forth Truth! Once you start seeing the real you, then you will see the issue that runs deep on the inside that you thought you had gotten rid of. When you get to that point you can deal with whatever problem you are facing. You must turn toward your reality. So many times, we run from our problems and not run into our problems. Embrace your life and begin to speak what God says about you and believe what you say. You first must ask yourself if there is a problem and accepted it. Embrace your pain. Say hello pain, I see you for who you are. The pain you feel today is the strength you feel tomorrow. All of the stress, trauma, and low lows you outlived. That means it could not destroy you, it tried, but it didn't. All of that happened to me, and it was for our good. You have the upper hand now that you know the truth. You don't have to turn back to the things you once did to cover up, and you don't have to run from it anymore. Your pain is a thin veil that covers the truth of who you are. You must know who you really are because there's power in your pain. The first step to **turning pain into power** is to allow yourself to feel. Feel those heavy emotions coming over you. Stop pretending that the feeling is not there. That is what we do when we drink, eat, smoke, and spend money; trust me it's more to that. The truth will set you free. When you get to a place in God and what He says about you, everything begins to shift. You can talk to your pain and say not so because my Father said it. We as a body of believers must become so Kingdom Minded that it would shape our life on earth as it is in Heaven. We are all special projects and God has great plans for us. It's a process and you will make it. Do not be afraid of the process. Know God for yourself.

Knowing God for Yourself

_____
_____
_____
_____
_____
_____
_____
_____
_____
_____
_____
_____
_____
_____
_____
_____
_____
_____
_____
_____
_____
_____
_____
_____
_____
_____
_____

What Is Your Turning Point

What is your fork in the road?

_____
_____
_____
_____
_____
_____
_____
_____
_____
_____
_____
_____
_____
_____
_____
_____
_____
_____
_____
_____
_____
_____
_____
_____
_____
_____
_____
_____
_____
_____
_____

_____
_____
_____
_____
_____
_____
_____
_____
_____
_____
_____
_____
_____
_____
_____
_____
_____
_____
_____
_____
_____
_____
_____
_____
_____

Are you Willing To Stand Alone!

How far are you willing to go outside of a relationship that no longer serves you?

CHAPTER 4

Looking In The Mirror

One of the most challenging things for any of us is to look into the mirror when our lives have been torn apart. I'm not speaking about a casual glance. I'm talking about when it causes you to pause and take a good look at who you are and what you have become. Before God changed my life, I had the opportunity to do that.

It was one of the most painful experiences I had ever encountered. Just looking in the mirror caused me to reflect on my past and I was devastated all over again. I felt sad, angry, hurt, and ashamed so much that I could feel the dark place and I didn't want to be there anymore. I was able to see the devil's work vividly. Of course, I couldn't stay there and continue to stare. It just seemed like everything that was wrong with me hit me in the face all at once. This was a very important step in my life. I had to come face to face with myself, now I can forgive myself. You must forgive yourself because if you don't you will self-sabotage. Your forgiveness is designed to put people in their rightful place when it comes to your life. The enemy will use people to attack you about your past, attack you as a person, your character, and your integrity. These are the spider webs that try to keep people tangled up and bound, but you're pushing forward today. You have to get to the place and say, "save your breath, there is nothing you can say to me." Save your energy because I'm totally secure in my relationship with God.

I knew I needed to change my life, since I didn't get to where I was overnight, I knew my life wouldn't change overnight. Romans 12:2 And be not conformed to this world: but be **ye transformed by the renewing of your mind**. That was the breaking point for me that if I wanted to see and do something different, I had to put it in my mind first. I had to transform the way I was thinking and do the opposite of how I was living.

Keys:

- You must be delivered.

- Turn away from the old way of thinking.

- Train your mind to do something different!

- Start Over

Scripture says we were born in sin, shaped in iniquity. Watch this, you have accepted Christ as your Lord and Savior, He has delivered you out of your sin, now you can start over and live a life pleasing to God.

There was a man that had an infirmity in the bible laid in Jerusalem at the pool of Bethesda, he waited for 38yrs to be healed. Whenever the angel would stir the water, he would try to get in, but someone always beat him to it. Jesus comes by, sees his condition, and asks, do you want to get well. People could see his condition, see his issues, see his sins, and would not help, why because they were in the same boat needing help themselves. Jesus tells him, Get up, take your bed and walk. Now in his deliverance, the Jews stop the healed man and tell him, you cannot do this, it is not right to carry your bed on the sabbath day. Who gave you this command to pick up your bed and walk? There it is the mind control. He was delivered from his condition and followed the instructions that were given to him. He left the old way of living and thinking behind him and started moving forward to live his new life of freedom. Now the devil is mad because another person has been snatched out of his kingdom and placed into the Kingdom of God. A little later Jesus found him in the Temple and said, you look wonderful! You're well! Don't return to a sinning life or something worse might happen!

I had to be delivered, I had to turn away from the old way of thinking and live a new life pleasing to God. For me to do that, I needed to know something, I needed to know kingdom principles. I realized then that if I did not roll up my sleeves and get to work on myself, I may never get the opportunity to put the work in. I want to tell you that your help is on the way! God is your healer and rescuer. Once He brings you out, do not turn back.

The mask was a shadow of what I wanted to become; it was my cover-up. Under the mask was the real person that wanted to live what was on the outside of me. The inner me was saying, I want to become my mask. My mask was perfect, it didn't have any issues or spots. The Mask was happy, and it never changed. This is the mask I made for myself. I created the mask the way I wanted to look and feel. However, it was also deceiving, double-minded, and two people at one time.

Displaying one thing and not the other. God does not want us to be double-minded. He wants us to be secure in Him. The Bible says A double-minded man is unstable in all his ways James 1:8. A double-mind is having opposite or opposing views at various times in your mind. To be double-minded is to be inconsistent, vacillating-wavering between two different opinions or actions, to be and act one way today, and be and act some other way tomorrow. Yes, that was me, double-minded! I can talk about it now because I am not scared or ashamed of the truth. God wants us to have a relationship with him and have a sound mind. He wants us to allow Him to come in and purify our hearts and make us clean, so HE can arise in us that His Glory may shine upon us. We can't keep deceiving ourselves, hearing the truth, and not walking in the truth.

You will never know who you are until you remove the mask. God wants to touch what is under the mask. He wants to fix what's been broken. **God** loves us so much despite all the junk we have in our lives. All of your weaknesses and mistakes make you a great candidate. Actually, you're the one God wants to use. God hath chosen the foolish things of the world to confound the wise and God hath chosen the weak things of the world to confound the things which are mighty. It's your weakness and mistakes that give you a voice. Your brokenness has a purpose. Look at yourself in the mirror! Take a good look in the mirror and what do you see? Take a pause and breath in and out. You Got This!!

The Mirror

What do you see when you look in the mirror? Let's walk in truth!

_____
_____
_____
_____
_____
_____
_____
_____
_____
_____
_____
_____
_____
_____
_____
_____
_____
_____
_____
_____
_____
_____
_____
_____
_____
_____
_____

The Mirror

What are some things in your life that you would like to
change as you look into the mirror?

_____
_____
_____
_____
_____
_____
_____
_____
_____
_____
_____
_____
_____
_____
_____
_____
_____
_____
_____
_____
_____
_____
_____
_____

The Mirror

What are some of your strongest qualities and how is it benefiting others?

_____

_____

_____

_____

_____

_____

_____

_____

_____

_____

_____

_____

_____

_____

_____

_____

_____

_____

_____

_____

_____

_____

_____

_____

_____

_____

_____

CHAPTER 5

Face-Off

Now as we come to where the rubber meets the road, I present to you the woman behind the mask, the man in the mirror, or whoever you may be, ...it's a FACE-OFF!!! It's Time to take the mask off, uncover yourself.

When I look back over my life, I realized that the things that transpired in my life caused me to live somewhat of a lie. I was living one way but presenting myself to the public and others in my family (and in the church) as another person. Trying to live the Christian life was so difficult for me at the time that I just couldn't seem to measure up to what God and others in the church required of me. So, I began to put on a mask. I lived behind that mask for many years pretending to be one way, when I knew in reality that I had some serious issues, and I just couldn't let them out of the bag. For many years I was a miserable Christian. I was praying for one thing and getting another. I knew that I had to change more of my habits, but I just couldn't find the will to do so.

About 10 years ago the Holy Spirit placed it on my heart to write a book about my life. The title of this book was given to me by the Holy Spirit and here I am now, years later writing the book that God instructed me to. Though the journey has not been easy, it has been rewarding. Living a double life is not easy. I would go to church and get hands laid on me by my Bishop and Pastor only to find myself in the same shape and the same situation, Sunday after Sunday. One day the Lord spoke to me and said, "You are wearing a mask." It was like He said, "You are wearing a mask and hiding behind it, and I see you, your Bishop sees you, your First Lady sees you, and so does everyone else." "Who do you think you are fooling?" I was torn apart. I was convicted some terrible and I began to weep. I was tired of who I was. I knew that I belonged to God and that I was saved, but oftentimes I didn't feel like I was a Christian. I felt ashamed of who I had become. My Pastors labored with me year in and year out, and my family and I served in the church faithfully. I served in about every area of the ministry that I could possibly serve. Our church started in our Pastor and wife's garage on the Southwest side of Houston, Texas. Many people in the hood knew the area as "The Clarke," that is, in Hiram Clarke. There was just a handful of us in the garage while Pastor Richard L. Holman was just preaching his heart out. I was the choir. Yes, little ole' torn apart me. I thank God for those moments because those moments made me.

The Mask

- Do you know who you really are?

- Do you know why you are here?

- Do you know your purpose in life?

- These questions are asked to identify yourself.

Every day people wake up to a life with no understanding of who they really are. No direction, just living. Living a Tiffany when we really are a Tamika.

Because of all the hurt, the pain, the letdowns, the let-outs, fears, and the pain of past and present relationships, we sometimes put on a mask to hide behind because we can't seem to overcome all of these pitfalls soon enough.

The things of darkness sometimes bring bitterness and unforgiveness, and sometimes causes us pain and frustration that we normally wouldn't have to deal with.

These are the things we don't like, so we put a mask on to cover up the black hole, or those things which bring emptiness in our life.

The mask is a covering worn on the face to conceal one's identity. As a disguise, the mask acts as a form of protection for the wearer who wishes to assume a role or task without being identified by others.

Sometimes, we (ourselves) don't want to be identified. Instead of dealing with the inner us, we prefer to deal with the outer us. It's easier to fix the outer us, nails done, hair done, face done, everything done. But at the end of the day, we have to face the real person. So why not deal with it so we can walk in freedom. God wants to bring light to the things that are hidden in the dark. God has determined as he said in Luke 12:2-3, that the secrets will be uncovered, the truth will come forth. For there is nothing covered, that shall not be revealed; neither hid, that shall not be known. Therefore, whatsoever ye have spoken in darkness shall be heard in the light; and that which ye have spoken in the ear in closets shall be proclaimed upon the housetops. What is done in the dark will come to light. He wants to expose the motives of the heart.

You need to know that YOU ARE NOT ALONE. The person that sits across from you at work is going through the same thing. That person that's sitting next to you in church, or sitting in the pulpit, YES IN THE CHURCH is dealing with the same thing. Sometimes the only answer people are looking for when they look for help is that they won't have to face this problem alone. YOU ARE NOT ALONE!!!!!!!!!!!!!!!!!!!!!!

As a child of God, it's important to know who you are and who's you are. Every day people wake up living a life with no understanding of who they really are. Depending on the occasion, we throw the mask on our face to hide the real us because we're so afraid of letting people see our shortcomings. When we are at work we put on a mask for control, at home a mask for I can handle this, and at the church, a mask for I have it all together. At the end of the day, we take the mask off and see ourselves, a mess.

We ask ourselves why and how? I don't like this place and don't like this person. You find yourself in a fight with an angel tarring all day and all night. All day we are going from mask to mask until one day something breaks. Jacob wrestled with an angel and in that place, God blessed him. You have to fight for your freedom. The angel told Jacob to let him go. Jacob said no, "I'm not going to let you go until you bless me.

You have to want a release. God wants to go beyond the mask and touch the inner you. God blessed Jacob during his breaking point because he struggled with God and with men, but he overcame. You have to overcome your hurt, pain, letdowns, habits, and the opinions of man. Your breaking point is the best place you could ever be. In that place, you find yourself with the loss of words before the throne of God saying, help me. God speaks saying, I can do it now.

The Lord wants to help you realize who you are. He's the only one that knows the real you. The only way you can find yourself is to find him. Psalms 118:5 says, In my anguish, I cried to the Lord, and He answered me by setting me free. You have to cry out to the Lord so he can come in and unlock the chains that have you bound. This starts at the breaking point. This place says enough is enough, I'm tired and I want better. You will never overcome something you can't face. You have to run head-on with every issue and embrace every pain. Whatever has you locked up, get freed. It is not you who holds you back, it's who you think you're not that holds you back. Who said that you can't do better or who told you you're not better? Why must we be so scared to overcome and become? Don't allow the enemy to play tricks on you, your life depends on it! Allow God to come in and set you free. I have listed a few people from the bible to share with you to let you know you are not alone.

You Are Not Alone

Delilah & Samson – hid behind the mask of his uncontrolled flesh... paid the price, identified with his purpose, bounced back from the filth and shame of an immoral and ungodly relationship with Delilah; made his way through blindness and found his way to the main pillars of the palace and destroyed the enemies of Israel (the Palestinians – the Philistines).

Rahab – respected the Spies (of God enough to cover them and hid them from the enemies of Israel, and it caused her to be delivered from behind the mask of the life of a prostitute.

Ruth – left her home and her people to live a changed life.

Esther – in exile, was promoted by God to become queen, only to have to forfeit the prestige of her wealth and influence in the King's palace and humble herself to identify with her God-given purpose and bring deliverance to the Jewish nation.

Naomi – allowed God to use her pain to position her back to her homeland and became a mentor to Ruth allowing her to continue the lineage of Christ by the will of God.

Sarah – a godly woman who is the mother of all the Gentile women in the New Testament church who will receive salvation, who by faith received the promised child in her womb, identified with her purpose after being met by an angel – became pregnant with the promised child which was an allegory of our Saviour.

Hannah – after being despised by Peninnah (the other woman in her husband's life) and being barren in her womb, cried out to God in prayer – realizing that unless she identified with her God-given purpose, her life would not be fulfilled; she defied the odds and went and prayed in the temple, risking the ridicule of the priest (Eli), and received strength to bear the child Samuel. Understanding the purpose of her own life, she gave the child back to God by leaving the child in the hands of the priest to be raised in the temple. She gave her blessing back to God in gratitude for a changed life and borne more children. The child Samuel grew and became a prophet to the nation of Israel. Because the mother stopped hiding behind the mask of feeling unworthy and useless, she identified with her purpose, pressed into the face of God, and birthed out her promise.

Free Yourself Today!

FACE-OFF

It's time to take the mask off, uncover yourself.

Identify Three Characteristics about yourself that would cause you to wear a Mask.

_____
_____
_____
_____
_____
_____
_____
_____
_____
_____
_____
_____
_____
_____
_____
_____
_____
_____
_____
_____
_____
_____
_____
_____
_____
_____
_____
_____
_____

What Will It Take for You To Remove Your Mask and Be Yourself?

FACE-OFF

_____
_____
_____
_____
_____
_____
_____
_____
_____
_____
_____
_____
_____
_____
_____
_____
_____
_____
_____
_____
_____
_____
_____
_____
_____
_____
_____
_____

Free Yourself Today!

Define What Freedom Means To You and How You Would Move Forward.

_____

_____

_____

_____

_____

_____

_____

_____

_____

_____

_____

_____

_____

_____

_____

_____

_____

_____

_____

_____

_____

_____

_____

_____

_____

_____

_____

CHAPTER 6

Finding Your Identity

Finding your identity can be an enormous task in our society. In general, we all come from what is a "dysfunctional family," and I say dysfunctional because whether you believe it or not, we are born sinners alienated from God and it doesn't matter if you grew up in a rich family or a poor family if any sinners were present, there was some dysfunction in the family. That is why finding our identity is a difficult task. We first try to identify with who we are by our relationship with our parents. This can be very difficult if we are not raised in a Christian home or a normal environment. It has been said by many professionals that growing up in a two-parent home does not always guarantee that we will experience a wholesome environment. Sometimes it creates more difficulties if the parents have some serious issues themselves with coping with life. However, no matter what the situation is in our upbringing, we seek and search for role models, we mimic our peers, and we strive to identify who we are through the family unit.

In this endeavor to find our identity we experience many pitfalls in life because the reality is that when we do realize who we are, and how we came to be in this world, the reality smacks us in the face and lets us know that no matter what has transpired in our lives if we want to excel in life, we better roll up our sleeves and do something about it. Identifying with your siblings (if you have any) and with your parents helps us to identify the structure of our generational make-up. In other words, we find out that the bigger scope of the world in which we have to do is much larger than the family that we were reared in. There is another world of beings in our families than the ones that lived in our home. Biblically and socially, we refer to the family unit as a generation (of people). The Bible talks about generational curses and generational blessings that affect all of our lives. Have you ever seen a family where the father has a problem with uncontrollable anger, his son seems to have been 'handed it', and the grandpa had the same problem? Or have you noticed that not only do you suffer from something such as persistent irrational fears or depression, but your mother and her father also suffered from it as well? There are many people today who are living under bondage that the sins of their forefathers have brought them under.

That means that in trying to find my identity I need to look beyond the members of my immediate family and look at the big picture of my family generations. In doing that, you will find that we all are affected by the sins and the blessings of our forefathers that are in our generation, and for us to make a difference in life we have overcome some issues that are a part of our generation as well as some of the obstacles we face in our family and our personal life.

Through my experience, when I came to know God for myself, I realized that finding my identity had a two-fold purpose. First, I had to find out where I fit in my family. I had to answer some questions. First of all, I had to ask myself, Who am I? Secondly, who did I come from? Thirdly, where did I come from? Fourth, where am I going? Finally, what is my purpose? Of course, there were many other answers to other questions that constantly ran through my mind, but these were the major ones.

After finding some answers as I went through life, I began to realize that God had a purpose for my life. This was scary at first because I did not know what it was. However, after coming to the point in my life where I knew that if my life did not change, I would end up in jail, in an institution, or dead. I knew that if I did not identify with the purpose God had for my life it would be over for me. After all, God saved me and delivered me from the direction I was headed in life, and I knew I had to give back to Him for all that He had done for me. Through much prayer and seeking God, I knew He had a purpose for my life, and I wanted Him to fulfill it because I wanted to be blessed! Hallelujah! I wanted all God had for me. So now that brings me to the point that I'm trying to make and that is, all of us who come to God come to the realization that we have to find our identity in **HIM.** Yes, in Him. He is our Father and our Creator and finding our identity in Him is just as important or more than finding our identity in our earthly parents. They both go hand-in-hand.

Once I found out that I was a child of God (after getting saved), it helped me find a new identity because I became a part of a new family. I took on a Kingdom family with many sisters and brothers. It was like being a baby starting all over. My thought process had to change so that my daily life could change, and that was a process. So, it took some time and little by little started breaking off my like. This did not happen overnight, it happened over years. You see, finding my new family and listening to what God says about me made me a new person. It gave me a new perspective because I became a new creature. Note, 2 Corinthians 5:17 states: Therefore, if any man is in Christ, he is a new creature: old things are passed away; behold, all things are become new.

Here we have found our identity and can find the answers to all of the above questions that I mentioned. You see, once you have made up in your mind to find your identity through your relationship with God through Jesus Christ, it is only then that your life begins to change spiritually, mentally, and physically. Having a relationship with God starts a transformation process that begins to conform us to His image. It not only helps us to find our identity, but it also helps us to identify with our purpose in life.

Life-Changing

The inner healing is a process that helps us to be who God has created us to be. "The real me." Jesus was my suffering sacrifice. He took my sins and gave me His righteousness, so my dead spirit could be born again. Jesus died so that we could have New Life! It was after I heard the word or the scripture, I trusted and believed in what I heard and that's what started the process of working in my life. You must let the process take root. In Genesis, we see God at work, and we learn how God intends us to work. We both obey and disobey God in our work, and we discover that God is at work in both our obedience and disobedience. You are not perfect; you are human, and you will make mistakes but you're striving for perfection. God knows this about all of us and He knows our end in the beginning. Catch this! The process has taken place in your life, but you feel like nothing is happening until something happens. Remember when you accepted Christ is when the process started. However, time, seasons, and moments bring life changes. Some people can have a life-changing experience overnight and some people can have a life-changing experience over time. These life-changing experiences happen till the end of time. Each change is always looking for the next change because the inner you are looking to become the person you really are in heaven. Yes, I said it, the person you are in heaven. When I found out I was already seated in Heaven, that blew me away! I'm royal, I have dominion, I have a crown, I speak with authority. Where does that happen on earth? That is how we should operate on earth. God wants us to operate from heaven on earth not on earth in heaven. The scripture says on earth as it is in Heaven. Psalm 139:16 Says Your eyes saw me when I was formless. Meaning before I was born. It goes on to say all my days were written in your book and planned before a single one of them began. Our Fathers knows all of us before we are born from the beginning to the end. You Were Made On Purpose With A Purpose! The goal is to get what was said about you before the foundation of the world to manifest on earth and get in place.

I Once Was Lost, But Now I'm Found

I'm now at a new place in my life where I see things differently. I think differently. The things I use to do, I don't do anymore. The places I use to go, I don't go anymore. The desire of the thing is gone. You may be saying to yourself, how do I get to that place. Return to the Father, seek His Face and He will do the rest. You just have to trust HIM. Go back and make Jesus the first, the center, and the Head of your life. The scripture says to seek First The Kingdom of God everything else will come along. You want your identity from God and not man. Many of us run around with plans of our own. We dress it up with makeup, eyelashes, and jewelry with a big smile on our face, faking it until we make it. I did that. But I have learned in God, you don't have to be fake; you just have to be you. What did God say about you? Remember God has a plan for your life and His Plan is Bigger than your plan.

As for me, I continue to keep myself connected to my father and grounded in His word, so He can help guide me through this through the journey of life. Even though I'm not perfect, I'm allowing God to process me. Each day I lean on Him, and life gets easier. In my good times, I lean and during the roughest times of my life, I lean. I couldn't have done this without my support system. My mother and father for loving me and taking me as far as they could. My husband, children, and grandbabies for loving me and stepping back watching the process take place before their eyes, and my family in Christ. Most of all My Bishop and My Prophetess covered me and knew me before and after. I am truly loved! Each person in my life played a part in my process and I'm still being processed.

It's not about being perfect. It's about being you and embracing what is inside of you. To live a better life on earth as it is in Heaven and to enlarge your territory. To walk in generational blessings and not curses. It's about knowing the power and authority you pack around every day because we are kingdom citizens, a royal priesthood, and a chosen generation. Remove that Mask and allow the Father to come in.

What Character In The Bible do You Relate To The Most?

_____
_____
_____
_____
_____
_____
_____
_____
_____
_____
_____
_____
_____
_____
_____
_____
_____
_____
_____
_____
_____
_____
_____
_____
_____
_____
_____
_____
_____

Name A Bible Character You Dislike and Why?

_____
_____
_____
_____
_____
_____
_____
_____
_____
_____
_____
_____
_____
_____
_____
_____
_____
_____
_____
_____
_____
_____
_____
_____
_____
_____
_____
_____

What are Three Vital Points You Have Learned From Reading This Book?

_____

_____

_____

_____

_____

_____

_____

_____

_____

_____

_____

_____

_____

_____

_____

_____

_____

_____

_____

_____

_____

_____

_____

_____

_____

_____

_____

_____

_____

_____

_____

How Will You Apply Them To Your Daily Life?